R5

POPULAR BAND

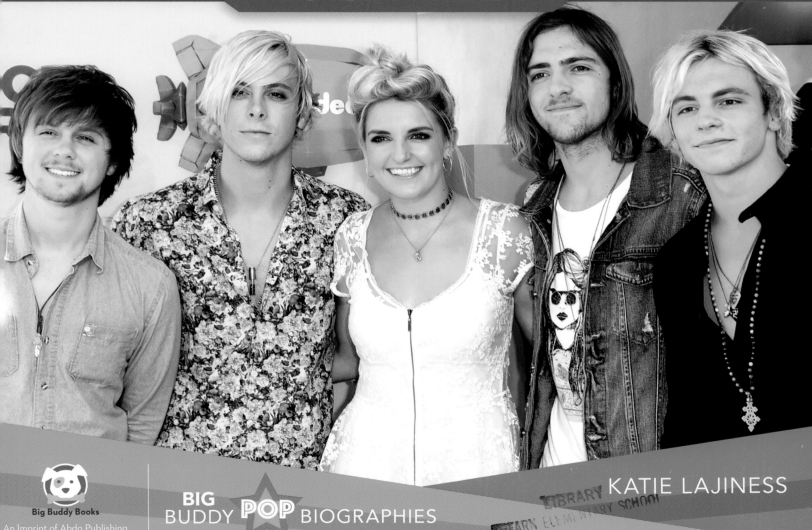

Big Buddy Books

An Imprint of Abdo Publishing
abdopublishing.com

BIG BUDDY **POP** BIOGRAPHIES

KATIE LAJINESS

abdopublishing.com

Published by Abdo Publishing, a division of ABDO, PO Box 398166, Minneapolis, Minnesota 55439.
Copyright © 2016 by Abdo Consulting Group, Inc. International copyrights reserved in all countries.
No part of this book may be reproduced in any form without written permission from the publisher.
Big Buddy Books™ is a trademark and logo of Abdo Publishing.

Printed in the United States of America, North Mankato, Minnesota.
102015
012016

THIS BOOK CONTAINS
RECYCLED MATERIALS

Cover Photo: Jason Merritt/Getty Images.
Interior Photos: Associated Press (p. 21); Barry Brecheisen/Getty Images (p. 11); Michael Buckner/
    Getty Images (p. 23); Larry Busacca/Getty Images (p. 9); Stephen J. Cohen/Getty Images
    (p. 25); Chelsea Lauren/Getty Images (p. 29); David Livingston/Getty Images (p. 27); Larry
    Marano/Getty Images (pp. 15, 17); Patrick R. Murphy/Getty Images (pp. 19, 21); J Carter
    Rinaldi/Getty Images (p. 13); John Salangsang/Invision/AP (pp. 5, 17); Richard Shotwell/
    Invision/AP (p. 9).

Coordinating Series Editor: Tamara L. Britton
Contributing Editor: Marcia Zappa
Graphic Design: Jenny Christensen

Library of Congress Cataloging-in-Publication Data

Lajiness, Katie.
  R5 / Katie Lajiness.
      pages cm. -- (Big Buddy pop biographies)
  Includes index.
  ISBN 978-1-68078-058-1
1. R5 (Musical group)--Juvenile literature. 2. Rock musicians--United States--Biography--Juvenile
literature. I. Title.
  ML3930.R15L35 2016
  782.421649092'2--dc23
  [B]
                            2015030702

CONTENTS

ROCK-STAR FAMILY

R5 is a **pop**-music band that formed in 2009. **Siblings** Riker, Rydel, Rocky, and Ross Lynch are in the band. Their friend Ellington Ratliff is the only member of R5 who is not a family member. Fans around the world love to listen to their music!

SNAPSHOT

NAME (left to right):	BIRTHDAY:
Riker Lynch	November 8, 1991
Rocky Lynch	November 1, 1994
Rydel Lynch	August 9, 1993
Ellington Ratliff	April 14, 1993
Ross Lynch	December 29, 1995

ALBUMS:

Louder, Sometime Last Night

FAMILY TIES

The Lynch kids grew up in Littleton, Colorado. Their parents are Mark and Stormie Lynch.

Growing up, the Lynch **siblings** did not always attend a school. Instead, the children were mostly homeschooled by their parents.

WHERE IN THE WORLD?

STARTING OUT

The Lynch **siblings** always loved to sing and dance. They wanted to be in show business. So in 2007, the family moved to Los Angeles, California.

To reach their goal, the kids worked hard to become actors, dancers, and **musicians**. In 2009, all four brothers were part of the dance group the Rage Boyz Crew. They were on the television show *So You Think You Can Dance*.

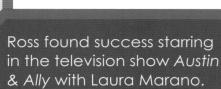

Ross found success starring in the television show *Austin & Ally* with Laura Marano.

Riker (*left*) got his big break when he appeared on the television show *Glee*.

9

BIG BREAK

Ellington Ratliff was born in Los Angeles. He always wanted to be a **performer**. The Lynches met Ellington at a performing arts **studio** around 2009. They soon formed R5. In 2010, the band **released** its first **EP**, *Ready Set Rock*.

DID YOU KNOW?
R5 got its name because everyone in the band has an R in his or her name.

In 2012, R5 played at the Magnificent Mile Lights Festival in Chicago, Illinois.

Fans liked R5's music. Then a record company wanted to record new music with R5. The band's first record with Hollywood Records was *Louder*. It came out in 2013.

R5 **released** the **EP** *Heart Made Up on You* in 2014. And, the band's album *Sometime Last Night* came out in 2015.

In 2013, R5 members went to Planet Hollywood in New York City, New York. The band members left their handprints.

FAN FAVORITES

Music fans get excited about their favorite **musicians**. They often want to learn everything about them. Fans share this information with others.

R5's fans were no different! They started fan clubs and **websites** about the band. Fans shared videos and photos on **social media**. In this way, more people learned about the band.

R5 fans often buy albums and attend concerts. Some fans make signs or shirts about the band.

15

RIKER

Riker Anthony Lynch was born on November 8, 1991. He is the oldest of the five Lynch **siblings**. Riker sings and plays **bass** in the band.

Riker used his singing and dancing skills to win television **roles**. From 2010 to 2013 he played Jeff, a member of the Dalton Academy Warblers, on *Glee*. In 2015, Riker appeared on *Dancing with the Stars*. He danced with Allison Holker. They won second place!

Riker's dance partner, Allison (*below*), appeared in R5's music video for "All Night."

RYDEL

Rydel Mary Lynch was born on August 9, 1993. She is the second-oldest **sibling** in the Lynch family. Rydel is the only girl in R5. She sings and plays the keyboard in the band.

In 2012, Rydel had a part on the television show *Bunheads*. She played a **performer** in Las Vegas, Nevada.

Rydel wears trendy clothes when she is on stage.

ROCKY

Rocky Mark Lynch was born on November 1, 1994. He is the third-oldest **sibling**. Rocky sings and plays **guitar** in the band.

Rocky was the first of the Lynch children to learn to play the guitar. Then, he helped teach Riker and Ross.

DID YOU KNOW?
Mark and Stormie let Riker choose Rocky's name!

When Rocky was a kid, he saw a music video by the rock band Fall Out Boy (*below*). It made him want to play guitar and start a band.

ROSS

Ross Shor Lynch was born on December 29, 1995. He is the second youngest of the Lynch children. Ross is R5's lead singer. He also plays the **guitar**.

Ross is the star of *Austin & Ally* on the Disney Channel. He also starred in the television movies *Teen Beach Movie* and *Teen Beach 2*.

DID YOU KNOW

Ross is featured at Madame Tussauds in Orlando, Florida. He has a figure that looks like him, but shaped out of wax!

Many fans found out about R5 after seeing Ross on television.

ELLINGTON

Ellington Lee Ratliff was born on April 14, 1993. He sings and plays the drums in the band.

Ellington has three half brothers named Elden, Garette, and Erick. All four brothers are actors. Ellington has had small **roles** on television shows such as *Raising Hope* and *Victorious*.

Ellington is known as the funniest member of R5.

OFF THE STAGE

R5 was in the **documentary** film *R5: All Day, All Night*. This movie follows R5's life behind the scenes with home videos. In the film, the band members also talked about their lives and adventures.

R5 has been a guest on many talk shows. And, the band has **performed** at events such as parades and **award** shows. R5 was **nominated** for the Choice Music Group at the 2014 Teen Choice Awards.

As rock stars, members of R5 often have their picture taken at events.

BUZZ

In summer 2015, R5 started a major tour. They did shows in North America and Europe for the Sometime Last Night Tour.

In 2015, the band went to the iHeartRadio Music **Awards**. That year, they also went to the Kids' Choice Awards. Fans are excited to see what R5 does next!

R5 is known for putting on fun shows. Its members often jump around on stage.

GLOSSARY

award something that is given in recognition of good work or a good act.

bass (BAYS) a stringed musical instrument played by strumming. It is similar to a guitar, but plays lower notes.

documentary a movie or television program that presents facts, often about an event or a person.

EP extended play. A music recording with more than one song, but fewer than a full album.

guitar (guh-TAHR) a stringed musical instrument played by strumming.

musician someone who writes, sings, or plays music.

nominate to name as a possible winner.

perform to do something in front of an audience. A performer is someone who performs.

pop relating to popular music.

release to make available to the public.

role a part an actor plays.

sibling a brother or a sister.

social media a form of communication on the Internet where people can share information, messages, and videos. It may include blogs and online groups.

studio a place where people go to learn or practice an art such as acting, dancing, or singing.

website a group of World Wide Web pages usually containing links to each other and made available online by an individual, company, or organization.

WEBSITES

To learn more about Pop Biographies, visit **booklinks.abdopublishing.com**. These links are routinely monitored and updated to provide the most current information available.

INDEX